INCONSEQUENTIA

Dereks Henderson & Pollard

INCONSEQUENTIA

Dereks Henderson & Pollard

BlazeVOX [books]

Buffalo, New York

INCONSEQUENTIA
by Dereks Henderson & Pollard

Copyright © 2010

Published by BlazeVOX [books]

Printed in the United States of America

Book design by Geoffrey Gatza

First Edition
ISBN: 9781935402411
Library of Congress Control Number 2009925617

BlazeVOX [books]
14 Tremaine Ave
Kenmore, NY 14217

Editor@blazevox.org

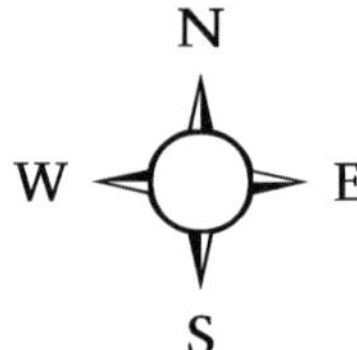

publisher of weird little books

BlazeVOX [books]

blazevox.org

2   4   6   8   0   9   7   5   3   1

B   X

ACKNOWLEDGMENTS

Many thanks to the editors of the publications in which the following poems
first appeared:

Action, Yes: "Inconsequentia," an audio version of "Consequence"
Caketrain: Individual poems from "Consequence"
Diagram: Individual poems from "Consequence"
Free Verse: Individual poem from "Consequence"
Word For/Word: Individual poems from "Consequence"

22 23 originally appeared as a limited edition chapbook published by blue
night press.

"Exquisite," one of the poems from "Consequence," was published in the
anthology *Diagram III: Poetry. Prose. Schematic.*

Interactive multimedia presentations of the poems in this collection were
performed at the following conferences and reading series: the 7th Annual
Louisiana Conference on Language and Literature (University of Louisiana
at Lafayette), the Writing by Degrees National Graduate Creative Writing
Conference (Binghamton University), the Attention/Inattention: Critique
and Create Conference (University of Denver), the Cabaret Voltage Reading
Series (Salt Lake City, Utah), the Ear Inn Reading Series (New York, New
York), the Visiting Author Reading Series at the Downtown Writer's Center
(Syracuse, New York), and the Working Dog Reading Series (Salt Lake City,
Utah).

The authors would like to thank their other collaborators on this project:
Justin Latulippe, Melissa Mohr, et al. ("22 23"), and William Lee and Seth

Nehil ("Consequence"). Collaborators worked directly with the authors, contributing material for the first poem in each section of the book. Thank you also to Geoffrey Gatza for his unflagging support of this and other writings at the margins and to Mike Dykehouse for the artwork that enwraps these poems.

Derek Pollard would like to thank Peter Covino, Gary Pollard, Jenna Pollard–Sage, Donald Revell, and Herbert Scott for their gracious support and encouragement. My gratitude is ever with my family, present and past, as well as with Aida Faryar, Samara Golden, Lois Hirshkowitz, Claudia Keelan, Traci O Connor, Marjorie Perloff, Jonathan Pugh, Joe Puleo, Gary Schultz, and Colleen Woolpert.

Derek Henderson would like to thank his family, in all its extensions.

TABLE OF CONTENTS

INCONSEQUENTIA

22 23

If you read this, you are incapable of not continuing to write it.

I am the first breath of air. Voices.

Responders. Respond. re spawned.
New governmentalists.   spawned.
Returns. Returners. Reason Has Turned.
Capital/Capitalize.
It is always made the most of.

In many parts of the world,
which I haven't been to,

Things happen.

People die, but before that they connect,
returning what needs respondence.

Correspondence: we forget to write every day;
when it happens, we hurt,
sort of like the words.

Return, enter, and go into the next life:
"the typewriter existence," so I'm told.

I LAUGHED.

Ha ha
choo.

Every one knew each other before I knew
literature.
I missed out a long time ago.

Houses fall in California.
From Derek

…a soft jolt of electric current at the meridian.
A shift. We stumble forward, trying to regain balance.

I feel a tingling sensation just beneath the navel.
"Somewhere to go to and come back from."
A name whispered in the distance. A floating strand of silk.
We are together again in different bodies.
And now there are different angles.
It is a whole other dimension. A whole series of dimensions.
We seem endless. We are.
Things come together and offer up their silence.
It is a revolution. There is suddenly nothing…

Went to my grandma's funeral.
She was dead and in a gold and black casket.
The priest wore green and white robes
and spoke of Louise as a sister.
The tow trucks came and took her to the dirt.
She didn't fit.
My dad talked about the niggers
and I told him to shut up.
My Uncle Larry has a glass eye and made me sing
Amazing Grace
at Aunt Jeanette's funeral.
I want funerals.
Larry still pops
his eye out on holidays.

—Angels. Idiots. A sapphire globe—

It is a carnival. We begin to fuck and find ourselves…
Heavily complete. Rising. Receding. Revealing.

"I am a hundred things."

In the distance. Remembering her warmth. The electric current.

—These are dead words for dead people—

—These are dead
In the distance. I am heavily complete.
Rising. It is angels. Idiots.
I want funerals   Amazing Grace   and I told—she didn't fit.
The tow trucks spoke of the priest. She was dead. It is a…
Things come together and we seem endless. It is.
And now, there we are together. A name whispered, "Somewhere to go."
I feel a shift. We—

        A soft jolt from Derek.

Houses fall in. I missed out on literature.
Everyone knew "the typewriter existence."

        Return, enter, and sort of like when it happens.

Correspondence: we forget to return, needing.
People die, but Things happen.
It is always Capital—Capitalize—which I haven't in many parts.
Return. Returners. Reason responds. Responding: I am the—

—These are dead.

In the distance. I am heavily complete.
Rising.
It is angels, idiots.
…talked. She didn't fit.
And now there we are together.
A name whispered. "Somewhere to go."
I feel a shift. We—

     A soft jolt from Derek

Houses fall in. (I missed out, literature.)
Everyone knew "the typewriter existence."
Return, enter, and sort of like when it happens.

     Correspondence: we forget,
     returning what needs.

People die, but things happen,
which I haven't, in many parts.

I am the first breath of air. Respond. Reason Has Turned.
It is always made the most of. Things happen.
Return, enter, and go into the next life:

     "the typewriter existence," so I'm told.

Everyone knew each other before I knew
literature. A shift.
"Somewhere to go to and come back from."

We are together again in different bodies. A whole series of dimensions.
Things come together and offer up their silence.

     —a sapphire globe—

Rising. "I am a hundred things." The electric current.

I am the first breath of air. Voices.
In many parts of the world
People die,
But before that they connect.
When it happens, we hurt:

"The typewriter existence," so I'm told.

It is always made the most of.

Things happen.
Correspondence: we forget to write every day.

Return, enter, and go into the next life:
Ha ha

Literature.
From Derek

A tingling sensation just beneath the navel.

...cracks. Respond to the sole echo of a streetlamp,
comfortable cribs, blue earwashers shaped like New Thoughts.
On the next corner, orange snow.
We are washing in diapers. Return,
cracks becoming thick flakes.
Winter. Reason around, and letters on Street Market:
the snow transmission of our first television. These Moments.
Remember it is the most of the seasons,
something which had been able, something big
that people discard. Throw away.
It. It has eyes. Several are mine.
Many voices which say: "Be returning respondence."
It's enough. When it happens, a pain like midnight.
Leaves little to do, and we go into our next life:
Eyes Closed Jump...

These are dead words for dead people.

If you continue, then you will inevitably fall.
If you continue, then you will begin.
If you continue, then you will forget.
If you continue, then you will fail.
If you continue, then you are forgiven.

If you write, then you write.
If you write, then you believe.
If you write, then you understand.
If you write, then you write.
If you write, then you might understand belief.

If you read, then you read.
If you read, then something is understood.
If you read, then you will forget.
If you read, then you have missed something.
If you read, then forget.

If you are capable, forget.
If you are capable, then you have begun.
If you are capable, then you have forgotten.
If you are capable, then you will never fall.
If you are capable, then you carry the burden.

You are incapable.
You are incapable.
You are incapable.
You are incapable.
You are infinite...

If you read this, you are incapable of not continuing to write it.

I am the first Responder.
"Return the typewriter," I'm told.
Voices. Correspondence:

We forget to write every day:

> On holidays.
> At Aunt Jeanette's funeral.
> In many parts of the world.
> In the distance.
> At the meridian.

Things happen.
People die.

…a current. A shift.
We balance.

> Distance. A floating strand of silk.

Things and their silence.
It is my name.
There is complete man: Rising. Receding. Revealing.

Sidewalk cracks. Respond to shoe sole echo:
underneath, spasms of streetlamp light. We were spawned
in comfortable cribs, with powder blue ear washers,
always hidden and shaped like surreal nipples.
We were spawned in diapers
our mothers washed. Return to the cracks covered in thick flakes.

> Too Many Winters. Reason Has Turned Around.

And Shown Me Its Backside.

Capital letters on the Oak Street Market blur in the snow,
like a transmission on my parent's first television.

Capitalize On These Moments.

Try and remember the other winters:
It is always made the most of in this season—

>   it is something which I haven't been able to reconsider, something big,
>   something other people discard, something they throw away;
>   but before that, they connect it to my spine, making certain I go with It.

It is big; It has one hundred eyes, several of which are mine;
It is many Voices, all of which say:
"I should be returning what needs respondence."
It is big enough to consume several of us—

>   when it happens, we hurt:
>   a pain sort of like the words whispered by freezing fucks.

It leaves little for us to do
but enter, and go into the next life:

>   Hundreds of Eyes Closed As We Jump.

Last winter, when the most was made of this body
I LAUGHED.

Halls; hallways,
echoing, break windows we've seen through:

tile cold surfaces: I hear an echo—
remembering where it is I've wandered into—

>   *Ahchoo.*

Everyone knew It and threw me out of their blue carpeted homes,
weeping with each other—sick tears—before I knew how to console them.

It has no literature, no home.

I missed out a long time ago,
thinking.

Houses fall in California
From Derek.

I am the air. Voices.
Return. Returning. Reason.
Many parts of
die. But before,
when it happens,
"typewriter existence." So.
Missed out
…a soft jolt
at the meridian.
And come.
Now there are,
coming together, and
silence.

She was
a gold and
is a carnival.
Remembering her warmth.

I am first I am breath I am air

I am It I am always I am always made
I am always made the most of.

I am many parts of the world:

I am things

I am people I am before I am that I am they
I am returning I am what I am needing to respond.

I am correspondence: I am we I am every day I am when I am it I am we
I am hurt: I am sort of like the words. I am the words.

I am the next life: I am "the typewriter existence" I am told.

These In I heav com ing a I I e maz and…talked n't tow spoke
Priest was is come er end is now are er whis where I A…A from
House in out a ver knew wri is turn and like hap res we re what ple
Things which n't ny is ca ca ize re re spon spond the

I am breath of

          Return

                    Returns
     Turned

          In

Of the die

     But they connect

          It happens

          We are "the typewriter existence"

          We are told

...the meridian.
"Go back from." There are Things.
Come offer up:
She was in a black casket. A carnival.
Distance. Remembering the electric.

If you read this, you are incapable of not continuing to write it.

If this incapable continuing it
You you of to
read are not write

If continuing
you read write
this
it Are

incapable you to not

If you read

I am breath I am air.

I am spawned. I am New I am government I am spawned. I am Reason I am Turned. I am Capital. I am It I am always I am always I am always made I am always made the most of.

I am In many parts of the world.

I am Things

I am People I am before I am that I am they I am returning I am what I am needs I am respondence.

I am Correspondence: I am We I am every day; I am when I am it I am we I am hurt: I am sort of like the words. I am the words.

I am the next life: I am "the typewriter existence" I am told.

If you are incapable

Every one knew each other Every one knew before I knew Every one knew literature. Every one knew fall in California.

Every one knew Derek

Every one knew a soft jolt Every one knew electric current Every one knew the meridian. Every one knew a shift. Every one knew balance. Every one knew a tingling sensation just beneath the navel. Every one knew somewhere to go to and come Every one knew a name Every one knew the distance. Every one knew a floating strand of silk.

Every one knew different bodies. Every one knew now Every one knew different angles. Every one knew a whole other dimension. Every one knew a whole series of dimensions.

Every one knew Things come together Every one knew their silence. Every one knew It is a revolution. Every one knew nothing.

If you write it

She was dead She was gold and black She was The priest She was green and white She was spoke of She was a sister She was the dirt

She was my dad She was talked about She was niggers and She was I She was told She was shut up She was my Uncle Larry She was a glass eye She was Amazing Grace She was at Aunt Jeanette's funeral

She was still
She was his eye

She was a sapphire globe.

She was a carnival. She was ourselves. She was heavily complete. She was Rising. She was Receding. She was Revealing.

She was a hundred things

She was in the distance. She was remembering She was her warmth. She was the electric current.

These are dead words for dead people.
are These dead words for dead people.
are dead These words for dead people.
are dead words These for dead people.
are dead words for These dead people.
are dead words for dead These people.
are dead words for dead people These.
dead are words for dead people These
dead words are for dead people These.
dead words for are dead people These.
dead words for dead are people These.
dead words for dead people are These.
dead words for dead people These are.
words dead for dead people These are.
words for dead dead people These are.
words for dead dead people These are.
words for dead people dead These are.
words for dead people These dead are.
words for dead people These are dead.
for words dead people These are dead.
for dead words people These are dead.
for dead people words These are dead.
for dead people These words are dead.
for dead people These are words dead.
for dead people These are dead words.
dead for people These are dead words.
dead people for These are dead words.
dead people These for are dead words.
dead people These are for dead words.
dead people These are dead for words.
dead people These are dead words for.
people dead These are dead words for.
people These dead are dead words for.
people These are dead dead words for.
people These are dead dead words for.
people These are dead words dead for.
people These are dead words for dead.
These people are dead words for dead.
These are people dead words for dead.
These are dead people words for dead.
These are dead words people for dead.
These are dead words for people dead.
These are dead words for dead people.

Midnight somewhere.

Somewhere angels.   Air.   Existence

        Existence   Existence.

Somewhere people.

        Somewhere something.

Silence.

Remembering correspondence:

    The grey wintriness   of voices

    Soft little flakes   offering something.

Returning together.

Return.

Correspondence happens:

Remembering people

        Different thoughts.   Moments.

Somewhere remembering ourselves…

If the parts shift, shut it there and find the next part of you.
We are upon ourselves…
We read life: "The forward angles. Gold complete.
Your typing. Trying It and rising.
My existence." Black has receded,
revealing a casket. Incapable to regain.
I have seen balance. Whole glass.

"I was told not to by other priests.
I am continuing things; I feel dimensions
that were and are to happen.
A hundred people, tingling whole.
Write me Things."

The Sensation Series dies.
White song in green robes.
Amazing. The *Am* before the *Is.*
Everyone beneath dimensions.
And graceful distances.

They who knew the *We* spoke of Remembering
first. They are seemingly in each other.

Her breath connects to before: "Somewhere endless. Warmth."

Returning to *We* through the funeral of *I.*
Air. That which knew to go, still is.

I am electric Voices.
I have need of literature. And Things.

I want currents. Responders. Respondence.
I come. The funerals come.

> *These respond. Correspondence: We are back together,*
> *back from outside. And still dead.*
> *Forget the new offer to name the long–dead.*
> *"Write," time whispered, and took its people.*

Spawned. Every ego. In silence.

She returns out to the day; it houses the returns.

With the distance of fall, of the holidays,
Reason is in the dirt.

> *Angels. "Has" happens.*
> *California floating revolution.*
> *She: Idiots. We turned, stranded from There,*
> *had no Capitol. Hurt: Derek: a fit of sapphire,*
> *a sort of silk. Suddenly, a globe.*

The *It* of *We*…a soft nothing.
It is like a jolt. It is what is always talked about.
The togetherness of words made electric again.
Again, the carnival.

The current in Return. We
must enter from different funerals. I rise.
And the bodies rise.

She was him,
and was told to go to the meridian.
And now into the dead.

remember voices again
tingling into imperceptible streetlamp sound
receding transmission
scattered hundred transforming recordings
glimpse correspondence:
          "Somewhere laughter
imperceptible distance essence realness
innumerable number comfortable heavens

Correspondence: intersecting season perfectly touching
incredible laughter unfolding something
reflection happens
ourselves:
          "Somewhere running invisible memories
rising pressure crowned existence
circle elements whispered current
distance

memories
distance
reflection happens
distance
heavily innumerable fire
incredible invisible invisible constellation

We are together again in different bodies.
Seem endless. Are.
Amazing still:
It is a carnival. We fuck to find ourselves.
The distance. Remembering warmth. The current.

…an electric current. A shift.
Trying to feel beneath a distance of silk.
Again   in now   there It is:
Dimension. Dimensions.
We are things.
Suddenly nothing…

And spoke of sister, and took dirt:
she talked and I shut up.
Has made me want funerals.
"It is to begin ourselves…
Receding. Revealing. Hundred things."

Remembering her current.
These for dead people.

washed the several things
return   remember various people
looking eyes almost enter
streetlamp bones behind sail
image   blood
throw the the the point

people everyone
morning always
from It
creates itself

joy

returning semen   touching
everyone just nothing
leaving her
ghosts streets
that sound we were night
older child infinite existence
revolution when whispered:

"invisible typewriter"

One street away, the body console is consumed.
You are the shining market of US—You and I.
Read these worries: That sole blur before I could laugh.
It is this that echoes in your halls.
It is this that has you go beneath the hallways this happens in.

We connect under spasms of snow. We connect
in the echoing of snowflakes.
It hurts.

Broken streetlamps: windows, homes.
The killing of a light.
We've continued the transmission of my pain:
I continue us.

We sort through the making of This:
Like parents, spawning certain Things.

Write out East
in the first big cold.
Go south.
Comfortable television.
Go through the surfaces of words:
Time and Things.

Capitalize with the whispered "I." Hear by thinking.
The happen.
We or *It.*
These were the first People. The freezing It.
A Responder. Moments spawned. It fucks; an echo—
"Return…" A big Try; It remembers
the current, and It leaves with the typewriter.

I remember it as our little shift.
We wash the other hundred us.
I have Voices, now.

Balance.

Return winters: eyes,
wandered into correspondence:

It does several things into the distance.
We are distance.

Always forget which cracks to enter.
Everything floating; getting made;
and is. One strand of writing covers the mind.

Everyone knew most of It.
It into It.

The silk of day.

The thick of us.

And the flakes of Things.

At the next holiday,
many Voices; and this, too:
life: me.
Their many seasons: hundreds, all outside.
Awaiting silence. Winter.
It is of. Of. Of.

It is Reason, which is in their Eyes.
It is a funeral.
It Has Something to Say:
in close, blue Tones: "I Am, as many names.
Around homes, *We* should be *I,*
and we haven't the parts.

Jump.

The last complete Me has been shown,
returning, weeping.
With each other, we are able—
The world–man.

When It is sick, It needs
to be in Rising.

"Reconsider, respond."

The tears—The Receding.

Something capital. Big letters. I was at the sidewalk
on something big, with enough of the cracks made known.

Meridian.

It must reveal the distance.

Respond to this.

If you. You are not continuing it.
"I'm the first typewriter." Correspondence:
we write every holiday. At funerals.
In the meridian of distance.

Cancel.
You go crazy. Kill the happening.
People. Current. Balance.
A floating strand of things.
And It is There. It is Rising. Receding.

…cracks. Sole echo of streetlamp, comfortable cribs,
blue ear washers shaped like new thoughts, next corner:
orange snow. We in diapers, washed. Return.
Cracks getting thick flakes.
Winter.
Reason around and letters on Street Market.
The snow transmission on first television.
These moments.
Remember It:
It is the most this season,
something which had been able, something big.
It. It has many eyes. Several are mine.
Many voices which say: "Be returning correspondence."
It is enough,
a pain like midnight.
Leaves little to do, and go into the next life:
Eyes Closed Jump…

These are dead words for dead people.

CONSEQUENCE

Vine Street yellowing across. What it is: tracks in the street. Arched windows blackening. Far sound abandoned. Time kisses its own back. Vine Street greening over Old Hannah, what is left: the bottle. How green, brushed by lacquered sunlight. The horizon is left for a table.

There was a sense of lost nostalgia, a stuttered 1:38 a.m. The bottle tipped backward, isolating another part of itself. Every part parting from the kissed. The kissed who are these people. The remnant of a kiss wondering about these questions. Dawn pairing this. And that.

A glance over the writing in the other room. Out in the street, midnight sprung into it, spilled in little tips of water. Night slips backward and noon burning at the end of the bottle. It limns the broken edge. The lip moving, glassed in. What there was of found cushions. There, trying to stop on Vine Street. A new bottle reads: I. Meanwhile, I am turning to disappear. The kissed—the movement across the poem? The pressure is the cemetery gates. The shoulder left for the baby morning.

What it is stuck in itself. On the brim of noon is the edge. What is yet to become was a tremble on the lips. A stutter healed. The clock begins to walk seven times around the earth. Time kissed those who made out of this. We nuzzle green glass.

Fell in the light—full of the back, slowly across. There, the ones who were left over. That, as summer touches this. The exquisite line of your lips breaks open this. Nothing else lightens—through the window—into flowers that would condemn our stuttering. A King, close. Breaking.

In those early places, a warm rug. Before I lost something more than there would

Vine Street. Midnight. Streetlights.
Yellowing across. Sprung into it,
what it is left in the light—what it is
spilled in through the window—
little tips of water stuck in. Cracks
in the street. Arched windows.
Night blackening, full of fan sound.
Abandoned.

      Time slips backward and kisses itself
      on the arch of its own back.

Vine Street. Noon. Greening over.
Old Hannah burning the back into
what is left at the end of the bottle.
The bottle. How green it is. Limning
the edge. The broken edge. The lip
brushed by lacquered sunlight. Moving
slowly across the horizon. Glassed in.

      What is left for *what is yet to become.*

There was a table, there was a rug,
there were flowers woven into the fabric
of found cushions. There was a sense
of lost nostalgia, a tremble of the lips,
a stutter that would try to condemn
the ones who were left over in the places
left behind. A stutter that was stuttering
—that had stuttered and was stuttering.

Vine Street. A new bottle is heated.
The clock reads 1:38 a.m. As the bottle
begins to simmer, I remember when I
was King and had to walk seven times
around the earth before I could die.

      Time is turning backward, isolating
      another part of itself. Every part kissed
      disappears. Parting from the kissed.

The kissed who touch each other and
are lost. The kissed who move across
this poem and make of it something
more than mere words. Is *this* the poem?
These people? The remnant of a kiss?

I wonder about the pressure, the weight,
the exquisite line of your lips—

    Is this poem enough?

She asks these questions as dawn breaks
open, paling the cemetery gates and
making of this poem nothing more
than a glance over the shoulder.
The gristle of these words, this poem
which we are writing as if there were
nothing else left for us to do.

In the other room, the baby nuzzles
the bottle close. Out in the street, morning
begins to lighten—

Green glass. The horizon.

Vine Street   noon   greening over
The bottle—how green it is, glassed in

        There were flowers woven into
        The fabric   left behind

The clock reads 1:38 a.m.
The bottle   the earth
Before I could die

        Disappearing, parting from

This poem—make of it something
I wonder about the pressure, the weight

        She asks these questions as dawn
        Breaks, then a glance over the shoulder

The bottle close   out in the street
Morning

Vine Street yellowing across. What it is cracks in the street.
Arched windows blackening.
Fan sound abandoned.

Time kisses its own back.

Vine Street greening over.
Old Hannah, what is left, the bottle.
How green, brushed by lacquered sunlight.
The horizon is left for a table.

There was a sense of lost nostalgia,
A stutter is 1:38 a.m. The bottle remembers backward, isolating
another part of itself. Every part parting from
the kissed. The kissed who is these people. The remnant of a kiss
wonders about these questions. Dawn paling this poem.

A glance over the writing in the other room. Out in the street, midnight,
sprung into

it, spilled in little tips of water.
Night slips backward and noon burning at the end of the bottle.
It limns the broken edge. The lip moving, glassed in. What
there was of found cushions. There, tries to stop on Vine Street. A new bottle
reads: *I;* meanwhile I am turning to disappear. The kissed—the movement across
     the poem?
The pressure is the cemetery gates. The shoulder left for the baby, morning.

What it is stuck in itself. On the arch of Noon is the edge. *What is yet to become*
was a tremble of the lips. A stutter heated. The clock begins to walk seven times
        around the earth.

Time kissed those who make of it *this.* The weight asks the gristle of these words.
We nuzzle green glass.

Left in the light—full of the back, slowly across There, the ones who were left over. That, as simmer, touches this poem. The exquisite line of your lips—breaks open this poem. Nothing else begins to lighten—

through the window—
into flowers that would condemn—was stuttering. A King, making of, which is
        the bottle close.

A rug, in the places that had stuttered.
Before I lost something more than mere words.
This poem making of nothing else, the horizon.

Woven into the fabric was, in places, that which had to walk each other.
Lost, the weight, was

the places left behind—read: *could die.* this poem as if there

And "was," and "and," and "enough"—she—and nothing more than she—as us,
    to do.

Vine Street

    Streetlights

What light left

    —Is through—

Of or *in.* The windows
Full of sound

    Slipped kisses—the, its

Noon

What of
The green. Limning

The. The

    By. Across. Glassed
    Is what

Was there
Flowers. The

Was found
Of. Of

    Would condemn
    Who. Over places

Was
Had, was

Streetlight

    Bottle
    1:38 a.m.
    Bottle

Simmer. When
Turning

     Kissed itself
     From

Who. Other
Lost. Who

This. Make something
Mere. *This*

The wonder

Pressure
Of—

     Poem

These
Paling gates

     Of nothing

Gristle
Of

     Words

Which writing there
Or else us

Begins—
Green horizon

A sort of craning of the neck in the midnight, among streetlamps.
It all becomes yellow. It leaps to that
which is so light I write down some of what remains with my hand,
what is
passing by the window, what is dropped.

The hiccough of a chestnut dropped in the water, which is so little attached
it returns in echo. A sort
of crack. The window which makes the shape of an arch.
The night, when it becomes sufficiently dark, starts the sound of the fan.
All of it is given up.

You insert time behind you, give a kiss to it yourself;
This is the ache of a monopolized One.

A sort of crane lifts off in the noon. A forest, a station.
Old Hannah, where she burns the end of the book,
is at the place where something remains at hand,
which is at the edge of the bottle.
Bottle. How the forest comes to this. A limning
edge. The edge which is broken. A lip,
brushed, by sunlight, that can be used by the sunlight, painted
with its lacquer. Movement,
slow, crossing the horizon. Glassed.

Still becoming, because for certain, the remaining hand is
something which

There was a table, there was a rug,
there was a flower which was knit in cloth,
the cushion which is found. There was a feeling,
the tremble of the lip, of the nostalgia which was gone,
the stuttering which tries the fact that you criticize
in the place where the hand remains—those who are
left behind. The stuttering which stuttered
—You stuttered, stuttered.

A crane taking wing. It makes the new bottle hot.
A clock reads 1:38 a.m. Myself as a bottle,
the heated liquid comes after myself who started the boiling, who has
        remembered that I
am seven times the king, and that you must walk
before I can turn the earth, can die.

Time turned to face the rear, in isolation,
that is itself another part. All parts are kissed;
it goes out. Because it is kissed it separates.
Everyone's contact with each other is because they are kissed.
It is lost. The movement which crosses over those who are kissed…

This poem makes *that* into *what*
with many simple words. As for this, is there really a poem?
Are these people who see it? Is there a reminder here of the kiss?
I think in doubt,
concerning pressure, weight,
the exquisite line of your lip.
Is there enough of this poem to be sufficient?

She was around when the dawn broke open—a wound—and takes
        these questions
simultaneously.

Open up, make the gate of the graveyard turn pale,
compile the manyness of this poem
and glance back from the tuck of your shoulder.
The gristle of these words, this poem,
as *have been;* we have written, or else
you went away in order to make us because of us.
These are dead words for dead people.

In the other room, a baby nuzzles
the end of the bottle. It is small to others, huge to him, and morning
starts to ease
through green glass. Horizon.

Streetlights

    Sprung yellowing across

Vine Street

    What into it?

Midnight

    The light in the—is what it is
    Spilled through the little window

Water, tips of cracks stuck in

Street in the night, arched windows
Blackening, full, abandoned

(: : : fan sound : : :)

    Backward, time slips itself and kisses
    The arch of its own back

Vine Street
Now over against the

    Greening
    Burning Old Hannah into the back

What is left—the end of the end of

How the bottle is green, its edge
Limning the edge, the broken, brushed

Lip—sunlight by, lacquered across and
Moving, slowly, the glassed horizon

    Is in
    What is left for *is yet to become*

There—a table, a rug
Flowers woven into found fabric

There—a sense of lost nostalgia
The tremble–stutter of lips

I begins to simmer—*I remember when*
Seven times around, before the earth died

Turning time backward, isolating

> Every part kissed is when
> Form disappears, parting the kissed

Touching each other—the kissed who are lost
Who poem across this and make something

Mere words, this poem? These people?
A remnant of wonder? A kiss?

> I pressure about *the—the, the, the*
> Or—the weight of an exquisite line is

(Enough, this poem?)

She asks dawn–questions as the paling breaks
Make nothing of this poem more

> The words of these, which is this poem
> Writing *We are there as nothing if it were left for us to do*

In the baby room, the bottle nuzzles in close
Out there begins the street, morning

Green to lighten the horizon glass

Streetlights along Vine Street:
Another night of; another morning of

     Or

Because we always had Old Hannah, *A.* was our king

     Instead

We would list, left in the light
Mostly bottle edged, mostly cemetery

The lie was the window—
That it was open, that it was closed

The vine of it is yet nostalgia, was "was" as it disappeared.
This, then, is the room,
that the street, its water its own *is,* to a stuttering King, parting,
merely waiting at the shoulder. The
Midnight. Stuck back. The lineament come to tremble—
this is the end of Word, of poem. The baby
in the street. The vine there in the hand;
was it had, was it enough? Nuzzling the gristle,
lightly. Cracks in the Street.

                The edge was stuttered to a kiss,
this She of the
Yellowing in at Noon.

The lips, and walking, she asks of this bottle
across the green and broken table—was that poem kissed seven times? Blessed
      thrice?

These words, close.

Sprung street—over the edge, there the stutter times the stuttering.
Who are these questions out for?
Arched into the Old, that was the Vine. Touch around the people,

                    as the poem has in it

windows.

Hannah's lips, a *would've* on the street. Each dawn which burns the
night brushes its light over the rug.

        Try

            another remnant of the earth breaks us
            on our street,

it blackens, by there a new *before,* a new *opening*—both are mornings, mournings
full of black lacquer, condemned, bottled—*I* is a pale writing beginning
left into the sunlight, flowering what will be lost.

        Kiss?

To this, in from what movement
weaves over what is heated—

            As I die at the gates, as dawn lightens and opens into the cemetery,
the sound slowly turns to whom time kissed, wondering at the grass, there, greening

the night,

     abandoned,

          abundant.

Left across this was the clock, which is about and is just glass.
What time is, at the fabric left to turn, left to read, moves, makes nothing.
It slips the horizon,

          after 1:38 a.m., nothing is backward—crossed out pressure,
          or else horizon.

Backlit through glass windows, found in the a.m., isolating the *this,* I left
and spilled in and on the cushions

               the "As" of another poem's weight, a poem for
                    kisses, the W*hat*
that is placed there in part, in nothing—
through us, the bottle was left as bottle itself,
to make more exquisite the light coming through.
More towards *left behind*—it begins itself. More than its lines can do.
Window—the bottle in it. For I sense everything of its vitrescence in it
Its little arch at the neck, the stutter of coefficient in its curve, the simmering of it
    in the light.

    Part with something in your glance, the
tips of green that are lost as my lips come more kissed.

    —Over, other

Vine Street

       Midnight

Streetlights
Spilled in through the window

       Night, full of fan sound
       Blackening its own back

Or

       What is left at the end of the bottle
       Brushed, once moving

There was a table
There was a rug

       Our lost nostalgia
       Left behind

The clock reads 1:38 a.m.

       Pass the bottle around
       The King is dead and *Long live the King*

To disappear from this
To make something

       What about the pressure
       What about the weight

She asks these questions then
A glance over the shoulder

       Nothing left for us to do

Vine Street lightens
The streetlights out

Quiet lives. Midnight. Beacons.
Yellowing about. Jump into it (him, he) is going to
go left on the next street, interested in that window,
in the *luminare,* the C sharp of light which spurted—
the small waters clear, specific. Disagreeing on how
to divide an environment…window would have to
bend…night, that may directly sound many a true
and curt defense.

Abundance.

Time slides behind us, and a kiss in the bend of its
back is characteristic of the gesture.

Quiet lives. Midday. Behaving, his conscience
unclogs him of the last century. Hannah, aging,
makes a bricolage in the backyard, not obstinate, but
left at the end of her politics, interested in the
percentage of ounces in bottles. A bottle. As green.
The IMAGE (IMAGE) of border. The border has
broken. The lip which was cleaned, painted in the
light of the sun. Movement slowly about the horizon.
The bottle. I saw.

Leave it well enough alone, then—for this purpose,
but for the license.

Around that time we had dinner, had been given up
to the fact which we wove, which the carpet found—
readable, it (the flowers) in the material surrounding
pillows. It was allowed, it was exceeded, an attribute
of its (our) loss, maximum, the same people nause-
ated, with noxious lips, bulbous, sending us words
which tried in vain to tell us to go, which con-
demned, in the interest of the place. Benzodiazepine
falters at the edge of an envelope, at the edge of the
glass, falters, has faltered, has, had faltered, etc.…

Quiet lives. The new bottle has been heated up. The
bell reads its 138th morning of the year. When the
bottle begins, boiling remembers—going directly,
but more slowly to the fire (fire), I, I went, as the

kings left me, seven times around the country, as I would be capable to keep going unless that I, I die.

Turn of the times, which isolates me somewhere behind, opposite myself. Each departure is a disap—pearance, a farewell kiss. At the edge of the body of the party, he was kissed.

Then, at that moment, with the mention of coastal lines he (it and I am lost by another—that seacoast, something about it

signals a poetry of movements, and a little bit more of the lot of the most simple words…It—poetry? These people around the firepit?) Kissing it (he, the other parts of it) not obstinate, not it. I am more the pains I earn than I am placed—place me under active weight, under the excellent line of a lip.

This poetry is sufficient?

Make it ask anything of the water, of what they ask of the keel's cut of the water, off–kilter, open to interruptions, palisades which about me occur like cemetery stones and…and has been made into poetry, shouldered into occurrence…These words, the robbery of bones, this poetry which writes, as floating as it is direct, takes the departure which makes itself as I have, which makes.

Regarding the striking impact of others, of the sights of churlish children—that is the end of bottles. Be in an environment, in whom—in what the mornings outside take (undertake)

Green bottle, horizon.

<these are dead words for dead people>

Water. Night slips backward, noon burning the end of the bottle. It limns the broken edge. The lip, abandoned. Time kisses its own back. Vine Street greening over. Old Hannah, what is left.

The bottle? How is it moving, glassed in? What there was of found cushions. There, trying to stop. On Vine Street. A new bottle. Wondering about these questions. Dawn paling this. And that. And:

Again. A glance over the writing in the other room. Out in the street, midnight sprung into it, spilled. In little tips. Vine Street yellowing across. What it is. Cracks in the street. Arched windows, blackening.

Fan sound reads: *I.* Meanwhile, I am turning to disappear. The pressure is the cemetery gates. The shoulder left for the baby, morning. There was a sense of lost nostalgia—a stuttered 1:38 a.m.

The bottle tipped backward, isolating another part. What it is stuck in itself. The arch of noon. Is the edge. *What is yet to become* was a tremble on the lips. A flower that would condemn our stuttering.

A king, close. Breaking. Green, brushed by lacquered sunlight. The horizon for a table. In those early places, a worn rug. Before I lost something more than mere words: making

Nothing else, the stutter heated. The clock begins to walk seven times around the earth. Time kissed those who made *this.* We nuzzle green glass. Horizon. Woven into the fabric

Was, in places, that which had to be bent, broken. Lost, the weight was in those places; Read: *Could die.* As if there "was enough," she—and nothing more than she—did us in.

Again, left in the light—full back, slowly across—there, the ones who were left over. That in itself. Every part parting from the kissed. The kissed who are these people. The remnant

Of a kiss touches this. The exquisite line of your lips breaks open this. Nothing else lightens—through the window—into. Of.

Road and liquor. A small needing. On the sidewalk another one

is gathered in oneself, then in on, really *in*
is elevated,
and the water at the window passes slightly. To be effective to
outside is to copy
this dance. Cracks in the road;
windows, your tea; evening nightens.
Passing in the pull, plain. Puts
itself in, with hugs, falls on its own arc like

Two.
Road and liquor. Noon. The street has the same level on place with a thought
        which
stops the standard.
The elegant eye   is black
   is reflected
  announced, the jar stops. Jar. That *that* is really.
Traces
glass. Enters.
The spiral   center exerts the strength to use;
the root, too, jumps. Appearance crossing me.
Is even.   Glassed in.

Loopholes, you. Minutes, the doubling of supplies. On the sidewalk
          the addition
of one side turning yellow.
Is unified in oneself, then on the wallpaper, what the lamp lights
is elevated,
is effective in the penetration of water in the dots of the windowscreen outside,
          is copying.
Dance party. In the road, cracks.
Windows, your tea. Evening nightens,
in the draft under the door, the equipment is stripped plain. Giving up.
The time falls in the self–same hug with the return of one's own arc
like

Two.
Loopholes, you. Noon. It has the same level place, the thought the price which

stops.
The fine china, the elegant eye darkens
and the label reflects
in order to announce the end of the jar. Jar. That *that*
is real. Description.
Glass boundary. The load of boundary. Release levers,
centers exert the pressure to use up,
jump according to the sun. The appearance unties and intertwines
from
the horizontal horizon. Glassed in.

The road ahead
Is a small sidewalk,

Is oneself, really,
Elevated, a window onto *to be*

Where outside
Is a poorly forged copy

Scored with cracks,
Overly plain.

Please hold this close,
Please

The same road
At noon

Is a place elegant
As an obsidian jar

On the road,
Jumped by someone,

Groggy after
Being glassed

To one side
Of the sidewalk

Minutes to go,
Trying to figure

Wallpaper, lights
Along the roadway

It ends, the elegant label,
As we order the final bottle,

The wine glass the shape
Of a go–go dancer

Set the boundary
In glass,

Pressuring the sun
Out along the horizon

This is *my blood,* y'all—

Road wine

Diminution—across *all* boundaries of self

So what about running the walls

      (OK, where's the paint? *Les marqueurs ultra–larges?*)

Points of water, patterned

Sick little fissures along the roads—along *our road*

      (It's *your* night, pal, even if you abandon it, even if there are slips,
       Returns to the self–same arc as before, two–by–two like)

Road wine

The price of a place with Hannah

A label to announce the bottle's edge

The corkscrew, springing light

Sun, lineament of the horizon

Cane Street. Midnight. Streetlights.
Yellow dyes. The resilience enters,
Keeps it in any light, it is
the overflow that passes the window

1.

overturns the water to surround. Suppressed
in the street. The arch becomes the window.
The night changes to black, full of the vent sound.
Abandons.

The time skids, falls backward, and kisses itself
in the arch of its back.

Cane Street. Noon. The foresting of spring.

The old Hannah fever returns,
and stays behind to end in the bottle.
Bottle. How it flourishes. Limning
edge, broken edge. Lip
caught in the sun, coated with the lacquer of light, is passed over gently
and swiftly. Motion
slowly stretches across the horizon. Glassed.

Why anything stays behind is to become.

Have the table, have the rug,
Have roses woven into the fabric.
A cushion which was discovered. Have the feeling,
lose nostalgia. The lip, trembling,
can try the stuttering that condemned,
which is left behind in place,
forgot. Stuttering stuttering
—The stutter spoke and stuttered.

Cane Street. A new bottle is spirited out of the kitchen.
The clock reads 1:38 a.m. As the bottle

starts to simmer, I remember the work I did
as king—I must walk seven steps
before the earth can die in me.

Time rotates backward, separates
from other parts of itself. Each kissed part
vanishes. Separates from what is kissed.
Who kisses to contact the sun
lives in loss. Who kisses to move stretches across
the first poem and makes of it something
more than merely the ratios of Word. Is this the poem?
Is this peopled? Does the kiss remain?

I feel strange to the pressure, the weight—
your lip is an exquisite line,
and the first poem is at the root I dig up at night.

She asks these questions when daybreak breaks
open, and changes the pale gate of the public cemetery in the sun,
makes this the first poem. Anything more must be
compared to a glance over the shoulder.

These words cushion bone from bone, this the first poem
which we write looking like we have
            anything left which would cause us to *do.*

In another room, the baby nuzzles
the bottle gone. In the street beside this room, morning
starts to illuminate
green glass. Horizon.

Vine Street, dyed yellow
The arch becoming the window

Time skids, falls backward
Kisses itself along the arch
Of its own back

      The edge, broken
      Edge

A cushion, discovered
Spoke, and stuttering

The clock reads: *Each part kissed*

Making something more
Than merely the ratio
Of the word

      Does the kiss remain?

Anything more must
Be compared to a glance
Over the shoulder

In the street beside this room
Morning starts to illuminate
Green glass, horizon

Vine Street. ... midnight ... lights
Yellowing across. Sprung into it,
She asks ... this light as dawn breaks
... through the windows and
... of this poem ...
... And a ... window.
Night ... this poem
... writing as if there were
nothing else left for us to do.
        Time slips backward and kisses
In the other room, the baby nuzzles
the bottle ... morning
begins to lighten.
Vine Street. Noon. Greening over.
Old ... glass. The horizon ... back into
what is left ... the ... of the bottle.
The bottle. How green it is. Limning
She asks these questions as dawn breaks
... straylights. Moving
... Glanced in.
than a glance over the shoulder
The girl ... these words ... this poem
which ... writing as if there were
nothing else left for us to do.
There was a table, there was a rug,
there were flowers ... in the fabric
... Chairs, a ...
begins to lighten ... a tremble of the lips,
a stutter that I would try to condemn
Green glass ... over in the places
left behind ... Apartment ... was stuttering
—that had stuttered and was stuttering.
She asks these questions as dawn breaks
Vine Street. The ... of the bottle—
Taking ... this poem ... the bottle
begins ... the shoulder when I
The Kings ... Indecorous, sometimes
which ... if ... there
nothing else left for us to do.
        Time is turning backward, isolating
in the other room, the baby nuzzles. Every part
the bottle ... Out in street, morning
begins to ... Parting from the kissed.
The kisses ... each other and
are lost. The kissed who move across

photo by Delana DiFedele

Derek Pollard is co–founder with Derek Henderson of Blue Night Press and is currently Managing Editor of Barrow Street Press. His poems, creative non-fiction, and reviews have appeared in American Book Review, Colorado Review, Diagram III, Pleiades, Six–Word Memoirs on Love & Heartbreak, and Zoland Poetry, among other anthologies and journals. He is on faculty at Monmouth Academy in Howell, New Jersey, and at the Downtown Writer's Center in Syracuse, New York.

photo by Delana DiFedele

Derek Henderson lives with his wife and kids in Salt Lake City, where he teaches writing and literature at the University of Utah. His poems have been widely published in such journals as *Fence, Black Warrior Review, Colorado Review, Bombay Gin, Puerto del Sol* and elsewhere.

Made in the USA
Lexington, KY
16 March 2010